THE *Miss*

CIRCULAR SAWS *and* JIG SAWS

{ the tool information you need at your fingertips }

skills institute press

*Distributed By
Fox Chapel Publishing*

FOX CHAPEL
PUBLISHING

© 2010 by Skills Institute Press LLC
"Missing Shop Manual" series trademark of Skills Institute Press
Published and distributed in North America by Fox Chapel Publishing Company, Inc.

Circular Saws and Jig Saws is an original work, first published in 2010.

Portions of text and art previously published by and reproduced under license with Direct Holdings Americas Inc.

ISBN 978-1-56523-469-7

Library of Congress Cataloging-in-Publication Data

Circular saw and jig saw

   p. cm. -- (The missing shop manual)

Includes index

ISBN: 978-1-56523-469-7

1. Circular saws. 2. Jig saws. I. Fox Chapel Publishing

TJ1230.C57 2010
684'.083--dc22

2009037454

To learn more about the other great books from Fox Chapel Publishing,
or to find a retailer near you, call toll-free 800-457-9112
or visit us at *www.FoxChapelPublishing.com*.

Note to Authors: We are always looking for talented authors to write new books
in our area of woodworking, design, and related crafts.
Please send a brief letter describing your idea to Acquisition Editor,
1970 Broad Street, East Petersburg, PA 17520.

Printed in China
First printing: February 2010

Contents

WHAT YOU WILL LEARN

Chapter 1
Portable Circular Saw, page 6

Chapter 2
Circular Saw Setup, page 18

Chapter 3
Circular Saw Cuts, page 24

Chapter 4
Jig Saw, page 46

Chapter 5
Jig Saw Blades, page 54

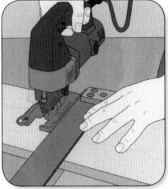

Chapter 6
Jig Saw Cuts, page 58

Chapter 7
Jig Saw Curves, page 68

CHAPTER 1:

Portable Circular Saw

Traditionally thought of as only a carpenter's tool, the circular saw has earned an important place in the woodworking shop. It is the ideal cutting tool for reducing large panels or long boards to a manageable size. Accordingly, the circular saw is often the first tool woodworkers reach for when they are working with heavy or unwieldy stock.

Imagine trying to rip a 4-by-8 panel of ¾-inch plywood in half on a radial arm saw or crosscutting 10-foot-long planks of 2-by-6 hardwood into 24-inch lengths on a table saw. Both cuts are certainly feasible, but in the time that it would take to set up the cuts and wrestle the wood onto the saw table, the circular saw could have already done the job. The only limitation is that you have to expect its cuts to be relatively inaccurate, compared to the precise results that a well-tuned stationary saw can deliver. However, in the first stages of a woodworking project, you are usually only cutting stock to rough length and width. It is only later, when the pieces have been reduced to a workable size, that you will cut them to their final dimensions.

Still, do not think of the circular saw as strictly a rough cutoff tool. With a plywood blade on its arbor, the saw can make quick work of crosscutting a plywood or hardboard panel without splintering the edges An edge guide will make a big difference, improving the accuracy of both rip cuts and crosscuts. Shopmade jigs and accessories will also help guide the saw for miter and taper cuts, and most saws have a built-in adjustment that tilts the baseplate for bevel cuts. Portable power saws can also make plunge cuts (page 42), an operation beyond the scope of any stationary saw.

Circular saws are designated according to their blade diameter. Models range from 4 to 16 inches, but the 7¼- and 8¼-inch sizes are the most popular home workshop saws.

Power is another factor that distinguishes one model from another. The bigger the motor, the longer a circular saw will cut without stalling or overheating. If you plan to use the tool principally on hardwood, a saw with a higher horsepower or ampere rating is your best bet.

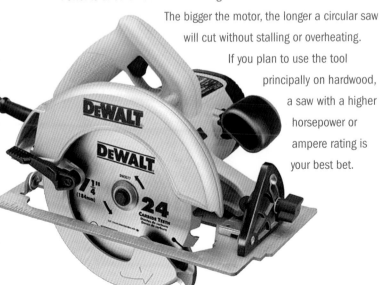

Even with its blade tilted to create a bevel, this 7¼-inch circular saw cuts deep to saw through 1-inch-thick stock.

Riding along the edge of a commercial jig, a circular saw can make a miter cut at a precise angle. The jig ensures that the blade keeps to the intended cutting path.

SAFETY TIPS

- Avoid steadying a workpiece by hand or propping it on your knee; always clamp stock to a work surface or sawhorses.

- Unplug the saw before changing the blade or making any other adjustments.

- To keep a panel from sagging in the middle and causing the blade to bind, support it all along its length on a platform of 2-by-4s.

- Do not use the saw if parts are loose, missing, or damaged; keep the tool clean to ensure the guards remain in good working order.

- Keep the power cord out of the saw's cutting path.

- Always wear safety glasses when operating the saw; because it cuts on the upstroke, the blade produces a shower of wood chips.

- Whenever possible, keep both hands on the saw throughout a cutting operation.

- Make sure the blade is not in contact with the workpiece when you turn on the saw. Allow the blade to come to full speed before feeding it into the stock.

- Do not force the saw through a cut; allow it to cut at its own speed.

- If the blade binds during a cut, do not lift the saw out of the kerf. First, turn the saw off, and then back the blade up slowly and allow it to stop spinning.

- When finished cutting, make sure the lower blade guard springs back over the blade at the end of a cut before setting the saw down.

- Do not attempt to cut through nails; this can cause kickback and ruin a blade.

CHOOSING A SAW

There are approximately 40 million portable circular saws in the United States. They vary widely in their design, but all models share certain common features; most importantly, they are powered by a motor connected to an arbor assembly that turns a blade counterclockwise. Depending on the height or angle of the baseplate relative to the blade, a saw can be set to cut stock of different thicknesses at a variety of angles between 45° and 90°.

When shopping for a circular saw, keep several factors in mind. Most tools range in horsepower from ½ to 2½ hp. Get a saw with at least 1 hp. For the sake of convenience, the tool should have a comfortable handle and a balanced design. Make sure the depth-of-cut and bevel settings are easy to adjust and the saw has a large, stable baseplate with both a long straight edge and a precise tilting mechanism. For safety's sake, select a saw that features a lock-off switch that must be depressed along with the trigger to turn on the tool. The two-step switch prevents accidental motor startup.

There are two main designs available for setting a circular saw's depth of cut. On pivot-foot saws, such as the model shown on page 21, the tool swivels up or down from a point at the front of the baseplate. The angle of the handle changes with the depth of cut. On drop-foot saws, the motor and blade housings are raised or lowered straight up or down relative to the baseplate. The handle angle remains constant, a feature many users find convenient.

CHOOSING A SAW *(continued)*

While the 7¼-inch saw shown here has been the traditional choice of most woodworkers because of its generous depth-of-cut capacity—2⅜ inches—a compact 6-inch model can also slice through a 2-by-4 at both 90° and 45°.

CHOOSING A SAW *(continued)*

Depth adjustment lever
Used to set cutting depth
of blade

Lock-off switch
Must be depressed before pressing
trigger switch to start motor

Handle

Trigger switch

Upper blade guard
Protects user from top
of blade

**Remote lower guard
retracting lever**
Conveniently located
near handle to retract
lower guard for
operations such as
plunge cutting

**Lower guard
retracting lever**

**Auxiliary
handle**

Wrench
For arbor
nut–commonly
stored on saw

Baseplate

Lower blade guard
Retracts into upper guard as
blade advances into cut; springs
back over blade at end of cut

Line guide
Aligns with
cutting line on
workpiece for
accurate cut

Bevel adjustment knob
Allows baseplate to be
tilted for bevel cuts

CHOOSING A SAW *(continued)*

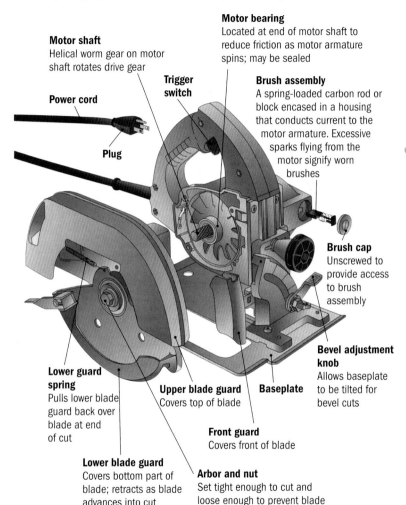

Motor bearing
Located at end of motor shaft to reduce friction as motor armature spins; may be sealed

Motor shaft
Helical worm gear on motor shaft rotates drive gear

Trigger switch

Brush assembly
A spring-loaded carbon rod or block encased in a housing that conducts current to the motor armature. Excessive sparks flying from the motor signify worn brushes

Power cord

Plug

Brush cap
Unscrewed to provide access to brush assembly

Bevel adjustment knob
Allows baseplate to be tilted for bevel cuts

Lower guard spring
Pulls lower blade guard back over blade at end of cut

Upper blade guard
Covers top of blade

Baseplate

Front guard
Covers front of blade

Lower blade guard
Covers bottom part of blade; retracts as blade advances into cut

Arbor and nut
Set tight enough to cut and loose enough to prevent blade from jamming

SAW BLADES

With the dozens of specialty blades on the market it is entirely possible to transform a circular saw from a job site workhorse into a precision cutting tool. Equipped with a standard combination blade and ones designed to cut specific materials, a saw can crosscut and rip accurately through hardwood, softwood, or manufactured panels such as plywood.

The cutting ability of a circular saw blade depends on several factors. A blade's hook angle, which determines how much bite it will take, is a key variable. (The angle is formed by the intersection of one line drawn from the tip of a tooth to the center of the arbor hole and one drawn parallel to the tooth's face.) The width of the kerf that the cutting edge creates is also important; so, too, is the number of teeth per inch (TPI). A 40 TPI crosscut blade will do its job slower than a 20 TPI combination blade, for example, but the finer-toothed model will produce a cleaner cut.

Although all of the blade types illustrated on page 15 are available in high-speed steel, carbide-tipped models have for years been the first choice of the majority of woodworkers. While they are more expensive than their steel counterparts, carbide-tipped blades are more economical in the long run. The small tips of carbide alloy welded onto the bodies of these blades can be sharpened dozens of times and hold their edge up to fifty times longer than steel blades.

But even carbide-tipped blades dull with extended use. Smoking, burning, off-line cutting, and frequent binding are all signs of a blade in need of sharpening. The best way to keep a blade sharp is to choose the right one for the material you are cutting and to avoid cutting into fasteners or accumulations of pitch.

SAW BLADES *(continued)*

Combination blade
The blade type usually supplied with the saw; a general-purpose blade for ripping and crosscutting.

Rip blade
Also knows as a framing blade; the large hooked teeth make it idea for fast cuts along the grain.

Plywood blade
For smooth cuts in plywood and veneered stock; small, pointed and finely ground teeth help reduce splintering.

Crosscut blade
For fast, smooth cuts across the grain; the blade's teeth are sharpened on the face and back, forming sharp cutting points.

Hollow ground planer blade
For very smooth rip cuts crosscuts and angle cuts; ideal for precision cabinet work. The blade's body is thinner than the hub and teeth reducing the chance of binding in the kerf.

SAW ACCESSORIES

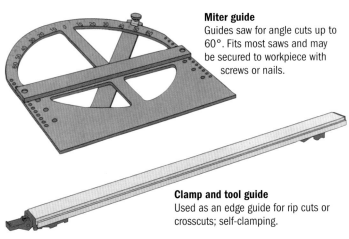

Miter guide
Guides saw for angle cuts up to 60°. Fits most saws and may be secured to workpiece with screws or nails.

Clamp and tool guide
Used as an edge guide for rip cuts or crosscuts; self-clamping.

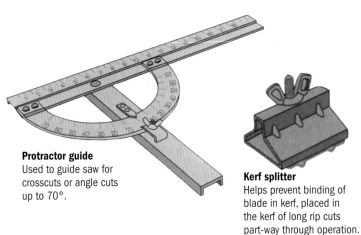

Protractor guide
Used to guide saw for crosscuts or angle cuts up to 70°.

Kerf splitter
Helps prevent binding of blade in kerf, placed in the kerf of long rip cuts part-way through operation.

KERF SPLITTER

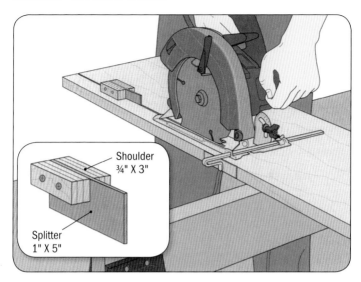

Shoulder
¾" X 3"

Splitter
1" X 5"

A kerf splitter helps prevent the saw from binding and kicking back. Instead of buying a kerf splitter like the one shown to the left in the inventory of accessories, you can easily make your own. Refer to the inset for suggested dimensions.

Choose ⅛-inch hardboard for the splitter piece and ¾-inch plywood for the shoulders. Fasten the three pieces together with screws. To use the jig, start the cut, turn off the saw, then insert the splitter in the kerf a few inches behind the saw. Pull the saw back slightly and continue the operation (above). For particularly long cuts, keep a few kerf splitters on hand, slipping them into the kerf at 2- to 3-foot intervals.

CHAPTER 2:

Circular Saw Setup

Proper maintenance of the circular saw blades will provide you with years of use.

CHANGING A BLADE

Unplug the saw and set it on its side on a work surface with the blade housing facing up. Retract the lower blade guard and, while gripping the blade with a rag, loosen the arbor nut with the wrench supplied with the saw (above). Remove

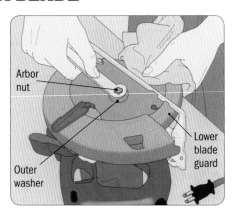

Arbor nut

Outer washer

Lower blade guard

the nut and the outer washer, then slide the blade from the arbor. As with table saw blades, carbide-tipped blades should be sent out for sharpening, but high-speed steel types can be sharpened in the shop. To install a blade, place it on the arbor with its teeth pointing in the direction of blade rotation. Install the washer and the nut, and tighten them by hand. Holding the blade with the rag, use the wrench to give the nut an additional quarter turn. Do not overtighten.

CLEANING A BLADE

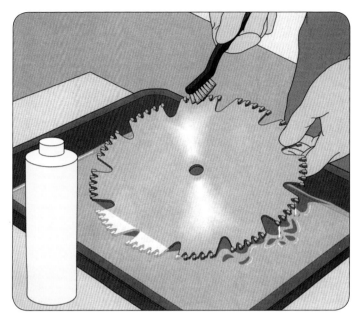

Clean the blade using a commercial resin solvent. (Commercial oven cleaner, turpentine, or a solution of hot water with ammonia may also be used.) For stubborn pitch and gum deposits, soak the blade in the cleaning agent in a shallow pan and use a brass-bristled brush to clean the teeth (above).

SQUARING THE BLADE

After pulling the plug, set the saw upside down on a work surface with the blade at its maximum cutting depth (top). Retract the lower blade guard, then butt the two sides of a try square against the baseplate and the blade between two teeth (bottom). The square should fit flush against the blade. If there is a gap between the two, loosen the bevel adjustment knob and tilt the baseplate until it touches the square, then tighten the knob.

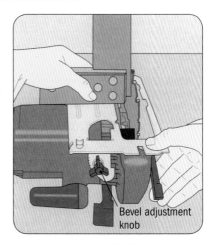

Bevel adjustment knob

DEPTH OF CUT

 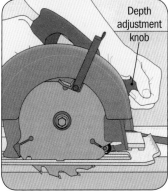

Depth
adjustment
knob

With the saw unplugged, retract the lower blade guard and set the
baseplate on the workpiece, butting the blade against the edge of the
stock. When cutting through a workpiece, set the blade to clear the stock
by about ¼-inch. For most blades, one tooth and at least part of the
adjoining gullets should project below the workpiece; if not, sawdust will
fail to clear the kerf, causing burning. For a pivot-foot saw (above left),
release the depth adjustment lever. Then, keeping the baseplate flat
on the workpiece, hold the handle and pivot the saw up or down until
the blade reaches the correct depth. Tighten the lever. For a drop-foot
model (above right), loosen the depth adjustment knob, then hold the
baseplate steady as you pull up or press down on the handle. When you
have the blade at the depth you need, tighten the knob.

SHARPENING STEEL BLADES

Jointing the Teeth

To sharpen the teeth of a circular saw blade, install the blade in a commercial saw-setting jig following the manufacturer's instructions. For the model shown, the blade teeth should be pointing counterclockwise. Install the jointing head on the jig, butting its file up against the saw teeth. Then tighten the thumbscrew

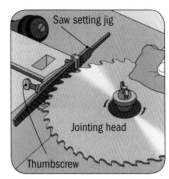

Saw setting jig

Jointing head

Thumbscrew

until the teeth drag against the file. To joint the teeth so they are all the same length, clamp the jig in a bench vise and rotate the blade against the file clockwise (above). After each rotation, tighten the thumbscrew slightly and repeat until the tip of each tooth has been filed flat.

Setting the teeth

Remove the jointing head from the jig and install the setting head. Also remove the jig from the vise and set it on the benchtop. Adjust the head for the appropriate amount of set, or bend. Using a pin punch and ball-peen hammer, lightly strike every second tooth against the setting head (right). Remove the blade and reverse

Pin punch

Setting head

the position of the setting head. Reinstall the blade with the teeth pointing in the opposite direction, and repeat for the teeth you skipped, again striking every second tooth.

SHARPENING STEEL BLADES *(continued)*

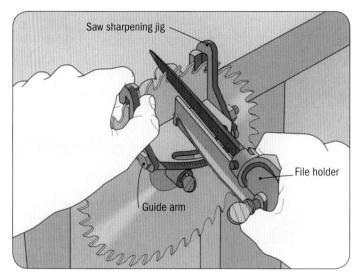

Filing the Teeth

Once the saw teeth have been jointed and set, file them using a commercial saw-sharpening jig. Mount the jig to a workbench and install the blade loosely on the jig so the blade turns. Following the manufacturer's instructions, rotate the triangular file in the file holder and adjust the guide arm to match the required pitch and angle of the saw teeth. Starting with a tooth that is pointing to the right, file the cutting edge by sliding the file holder along the top of the jig (above). Rotate the blade counterclockwise, skipping one tooth, and repeat. Sharpen all of the right-pointing teeth the same way. Adjust the triangular file and the guide arm to work on the left-pointing teeth and repeat, sharpening all of the teeth you skipped.

CHAPTER 3:

Circular Saw Cuts

Careful use of the circular saw can provide you with both rough and fine cuts.

BASIC CUTS

Whether you are crosscutting a narrow board or ripping a sheet of plywood, always protect yourself from kickback by using C-clamps and protective wood pads to clamp stock to a work surface before cutting it with a circular saw. Other safeguards include keeping blades clean, setting the cutting depth no deeper than you need, and making sure your stock is dry and free of any fasteners. To get accurate results, cut with the blade just to the waste side of the cutting line and use an edge guide.

Get in the habit of cutting face down because circular saw blades cut on the upstroke. If you are working with hardwood or veneered plywood, which has two good faces, score with a utility knife before making the cut.

Some commercial guides can be extended up to 8 feet. The one shown at left is more suitable for crosscutting. It features clamps underneath the guide that secure the device to a workpiece, eliminating the need for separate clamps.

CROSSCUT TO LENGTH

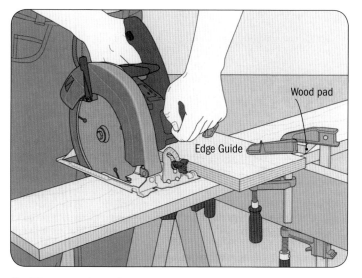

Wood pad

Edge Guide

Cutting stock to length

Clamp the workpiece to sawhorses. Align the blade with the cutting
line, then clamp a straightedge guide to the workpiece flush against
the saw's baseplate. The guide should be longer than the width of the
workpiece and square to the edges of the stock. Take care also to set
up the clamps so that they will not interfere with the motor as you make
the cut. Turn on the saw with the baseplate flush against the guide and
the blade clear of the stock. Then, gripping the handles firmly with both
hands, feed the saw steadily into the workpiece.

CROSSCUTTING JIG

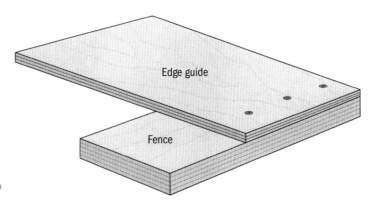

Edge guide

Fence

Simple to make, the shop-built jig shown above will ensure your crosscuts are square to the edges of the stock. Select ½-inch plywood for the edge guide and ¾-inch plywood for the fence. The dimensions of the jig depend on the width of the stock you will be cutting and the width of your saw's baseplate.

Make the edge guide at least as long as the width of your workpiece and wide enough to clamp to the board without getting in the way of the saw as you are making the cut. The fence should be about 4 inches wide and longer than the combined width of the edge guide and the baseplate of the saw. Screw the two parts of the jig together, checking with a try square to make sure that they are perfectly perpendicular.

CROSSCUTTING JIG *(continued)*

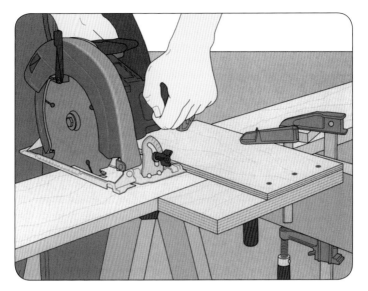

To use the jig, clamp it to the workpiece as you would for a standard crosscut (page 25), making sure the blade is held in alignment with the cutting mark on the workpiece. The fence should always be kept flush against the edge of the workpiece. Run the saw along the edge guide to make the cut. (The first use of the jig will immediately trim the end of the fence flush with the blade.)

For subsequent cuts, clamp the jig to the workpiece, aligning the end of the fence with the cutting mark on your stock.

RIPPING TO WIDTH

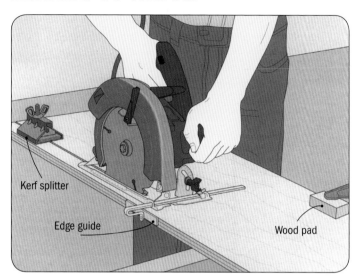

Kerf splitter

Edge guide

Wood pad

Install a commercial edge guide on the saw, then align the blade with the cutting line on the board. Butt the edge guide's fence against the edge of the workpiece, then lock it in place. Holding the saw firmly, feed the blade into the board, keeping the edge guide fence flush against the stock. To prevent the blade from binding in a long workpiece, turn off the saw a few inches into the cut and insert a kerf splitter. Pull the saw back a bit, then turn it on and continue the cut.

REFERENCE MARKS

Some saws do not provide reference marks to help you align the blade with a cutting line on a workpiece; other machines have lines that may not be perfectly aligned for a particular saw blade. Solve the problem by adding your own marks. Cut into a scrap board, then back the saw partly out of the kerf and unplug the machine. Make a mark on the toe of the baseplate in line with the kerf, then fix a strip of masking tape on the toe, aligning its edge with the mark. Use the same procedure to make additional marks for angle cuts.

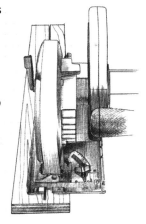

ShopTip

Avoid Splintering

Plywood is particularly prone to splintering when cut with a circular saw. A plywood blade will help, but another solution is to reinforce the wood surface with a strip of masking tape. Mark the cutting line on the tape and make the cut. The tape will keep the edges of the kerf clean.

SAWING PLYWOOD

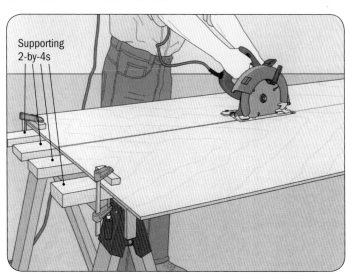

Supporting
2-by-4s

Ripping

To prevent a panel from sagging in the middle during a cut and causing
the blade to bind, support the stock on a platform of sawhorses and
2-by-4s as shown at left. Make sure that two of the boards will be about
3 inches on either side of the cutting line. Position the panel on the
2-by-4s and clamp it in place. For extra accuracy, clamp a straightedge
guide to the panel (page 25). Aligning the blade with the cutting line,
cut slowly and steadily while guiding the saw with both hands. Insert kerf
splitters as you go to keep the blade from binding.

SAWING PLYWOOD *(continued)*

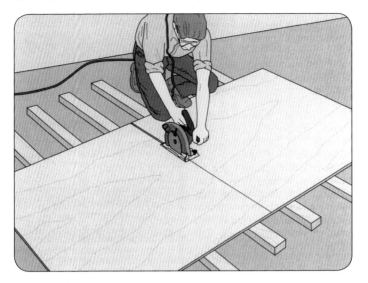

Crosscutting

Set enough 2-by-4s face up on the shop floor to support the panel at 12-inch intervals; the boards should be a few feet longer than the width of the panel. Position the stock on the boards, shifting two of them to rest about 3 inches on either side of the cutting line. To make the cut, drop to one knee and align the blade with the cutting mark. Gripping the saw with both hands, cut steadily while carefully maintaining your balance (above). As much as possible, keep your weight on the 2-by-4 immediately to the side of the cutting line, rather than on the panel itself.

STRAIGHTEDGE GUIDE

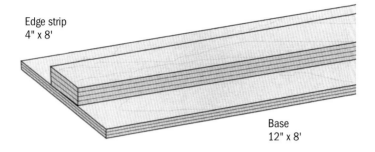

Edge strip
4" x 8'

Base
12" x 8'

The shop-built straightedge guide shown above makes it easy to rip manufactured panels like plywood with great accuracy. Refer to the illustration for suggested dimensions.

Make the base from ¼-inch plywood; use ¾-inch plywood for the edge strip. Glue the strip parallel to the base, offsetting its edge about 4 inches in from one edge of the base. Trim the base to its proper width for your saw by butting the tool's baseplate against the jig's edge strip and cutting along the base.

STRAIGHTEDGE GUIDE *(continued)*

To use the jig, make a cutting mark on the panel, then clamp the stock to a platform of 2-by-4s resting sturdily atop sawhorses. Clamp the guide to the panel, aligning the trimmed edge of the base with the mark on the workpiece.

Make the cut as you would a standard rip cut (page 26), keeping the saw's baseplate flush against the edge strip throughout the operation (above).

THICK WOOD

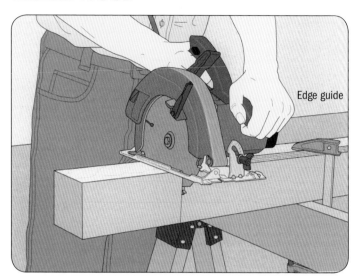

Edge guide

To crosscut stock thicker than the maximum blade depth of your saw, make intersecting cuts from opposite sides of the workpiece. First, mark a cutting line on one face of the stock, then use a try square to extend the line around the other three faces. Set the workpiece on sawhorses and clamp it in position. Align the blade with the cutting line, then butt an edge guide against the saw's baseplate and clamp it to the workpiece. Set the cutting depth at slightly more than one-half the thickness of the stock, then make the cut (above). Flip the workpiece over, reposition the clamps and the edge guide, then complete the cut.

ANGLES

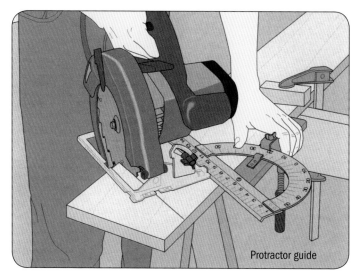

Protractor guide

Clamp the workpiece to sawhorses, then set a protractor guide or a miter guide to the angle you wish to cut. Align the saw blade with the cutting line on the work-piece. Place the protractor on the stock, holding its guiding edge against the saw's baseplate and its fence against the edge of the workpiece. Grasp the saw and the guide firmly while you are making the cut.

BEVELS

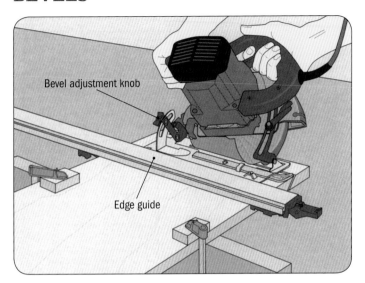

Bevel adjustment knob

Edge guide

Making a bevel cut

Loosen the bevel adjustment knob on the saw and set the blade to the desired angle, then tighten the knob. Clamp the workpiece to sawhorses, making sure nothing is in the way of the blade during the cut. Align the blade with the cutting mark, then butt an edge guide flush against the saw's baseplate. Clamp the guide to the board. Make the cut as you would a standard crosscut, holding the saw firmly with both hands and keeping the baseplate flat on the workpiece.

TAPERS

Edge guide

Cutting a taper

Set the stock on a work surface with the cutting line extending several inches off the edge. Position the workpiece so you will be able to start the cut at the end of the board, rather than on its edge. Line up the blade with the cutting mark, then clamp an edge guide on top of the stock flush against the saw's baseplate; measure, if necessary, to make sure the guide is parallel to the line. Make the cut as you would a standard rip cut. Keep a firm hold on the saw, especially near the end of the cut, when the waste section supporting the tool becomes progressively narrower.

MITER GUIDE

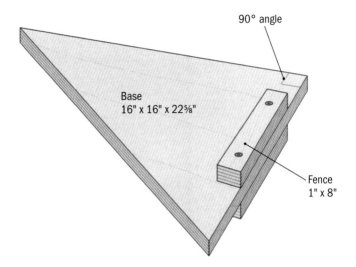

90° angle

Base
16" x 16" x 22⅝"

Fence
1" x 8"

Cut a triangle with one 90° angle and two 45° angles. (To make a jig for 30° or 60° angles, the sides should be 12, 16, and 20 inches—or any other variation with a 3-4-5 ratio.) Screw the fences to the base, one on each side, opposite one of the 45° angles. The fences must be flush with the edge of the jig base.

MITER GUIDE *(continued)*

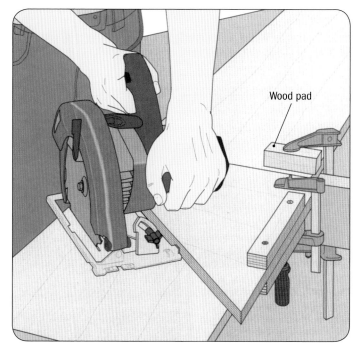

Wood pad

To use the jig for a miter cut, first clamp the workpiece to sawhorses. Then align the blade of the saw with the cutting line on the stock and butt the long side of the jig against the saw's baseplate. Place the fence on the bottom of the guide flush against the workpiece. Clamp the jig in place, and make the cut as you would a standard miter. Keep the saw flush against the jig throughout the operation. To make a crosscut, use the other side of the jig as your guide.

DADOES

Saw Kerfs

A little ingenuity—along with the appropriate jigs and setups—greatly expands the versatility of a circular saw. Although the tool is not a substitute for a table saw, it does more than simple dimensioning of stock. Dadoes, rabbets, and miters can be formed with precision approaching that of a stationary saw. For cleaner results and less tearout, use a fine-tooth blade when performing such tasks.

Although the circular saw may not always cut wood as quickly as the table saw, the tool's portability allows it to work in places off limits to stationary machines. The saw can plunge into the middle of a panel, for example, cutting a rectangular hole out of it while leaving the edges intact.

Cutting kerfs within the dado outline

Mark the width of the dado on the face of the stock, then clamp it to a work surface. Mark a depth line on the edge of the workpiece as a reference point and set the cutting depth of the blade appropriately. Align the blade

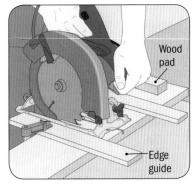

Wood pad

Edge guide

with one of the width marks and clamp an edge guide in place. Repeat for the other side of the dado. Gripping the saw firmly, ride the baseplate along one guide to cut an edge of the dado. Then run the saw along the second support to cut the channel's other edge (above). Saw a number of kerfs between the two cuts, working at roughly ⅛-inch intervals.

DADOES *(continued)*

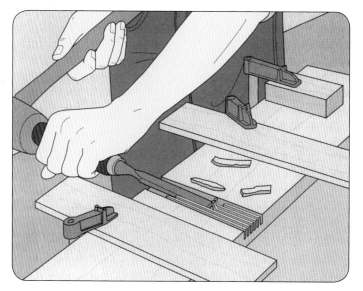

Chisel the Waste

Holding a wood chisel at a slight angle as shown, strike the handle with a wooden mallet to split off the ridges between the edges of the dado (above). Make sure the beveled side of the chisel is facing up. After the bulk of the waste has been removed, pare away at the bottom of the dado until it is smooth and flat.

PLUNGE CUT

Starting the Cut

Clamp the workpiece to sawhorses and align the blade with one of the cutting lines. Then clamp an edge guide to the workpiece flush against the baseplate of the saw. Make the guide longer than the cutting mark and high enough to guide the saw when it is tilted up. Retracting the lower blade guard with one hand and

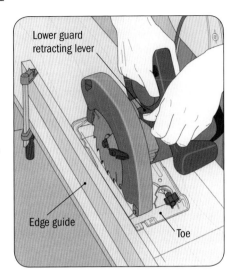

Lower guard retracting lever

Edge guide

Toe

gripping the handle firmly with the other, rest the toe of the baseplate on the workpiece and pivot the saw forward to raise the blade completely clear of the stock. With the back of the blade directly above the start of the cutting line, turn on the saw and slowly lower the cutting edge into the stock (above), keeping the baseplate flush against the edge guide. Once the saw is flat on the workpiece, release the blade guard and push the tool forward. When the blade reaches the end of the cutting line, turn off the saw, let the blade stop, and pivot the tool forward to lift it out of the kerf. Make plunge cuts along the three remaining cutting lines, repositioning the edge guide as necessary.

PLUNGE CUT *(continued)*

Completing the Cut

Because of its circular blade, a portable power saw leaves a small amount of waste at the beginning and end of each plunge cut. Square the corners with a saber saw or a handsaw (above), making sure you keep the blade vertical as you cut.

EXTEND THE EDGE GUIDE

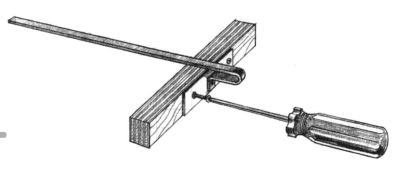

Commercial edge guides are often too short to provide proper support, especially for long rip cuts. One answer is to make the guide longer. Cut an 8-inch-long strip of ¾-inch plywood. Drill two screw holes through the edge guide's fence, then secure the auxiliary guide in place.

REDUCE SPLINTERING

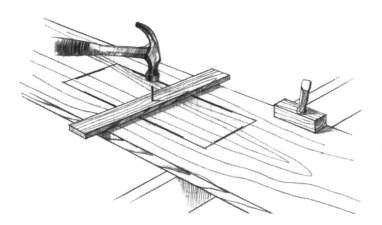

Letting the waste piece sag and finally fall to the shop floor when the last cut detaches it from your workpiece invariably results in splintering of the cut edges. Get cleaner plunge cuts by laying a board across the stock and nailing it to the waste piece before making the final cut. Then lift out the waste piece without marring the edges of the cutout.

Jig Saw

The jig (or saber) saw is often likened to its larger shop cousin, the band saw.

Although few woodworkers would consider using the portable tool to resaw a hardwood plank or carve out a cabriole leg, the comparison is apt in other ways. With its relatively narrow blade, the jig saw makes straight and curved cuts with equal ease and accuracy. Aided by commercial or shopmade jigs, it carves out a perfect circle. And like the band saw, the jig saw cuts identical copies of a curved pattern.

In certain situations, a portable saw can be a better choice than its stationary counterpart. If you are working with a long board or wide panel that requires a time-consuming setup on a saw table, it is sometimes simpler to carry the jig saw to the work for a quick cut. Because one end of the blade is free, the cutting edge can be plunged into a workpiece for interior cuts on which a band saw would have to begin at the edge of the stock.

The jig saw has come a long way since its introduction. Woodworkers complained that the first generation of saws were plagued by inconsistent motor speeds and blades that tended to bend, making it difficult to follow a cutting line. The newest models feature electronic motors that can maintain a constant speed under changing load conditions. And blade manufacturers offer a variety of sturdy blades suitable for any situation.

Making precise, splinter-free cuts requires attention to several factors. A key variable is choosing the best blade for the job (page 54). For straight and angled cuts, an edge guide assists greatly in keeping the blade in line. Because the jig saw blade cuts on the upstroke, there is a tendency for splintering to occur on the top face of a workpiece. One way to counteract this problem is to slow the cut rate. Remember to buff the bottom of your saw's baseplate occasionally with steel wool to remove dirt, grime, and burrs that could scratch the workpiece.

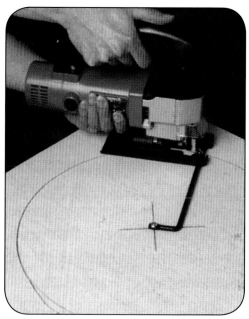

With the help of a commercial circle-cutting jig, a saber saw completes a perfect 360° cut in a piece of ¾-inch plywood. To reduce splintering on the outside surface of the stock, this piece was clamped with its best face down.

4: JIG SAW

There is no prescribed way to grip a jig saw. The manner in which you handle the tool depends on the design of your particular model. Many cuts can be performed with one hand on the handle squeezing the trigger and the other hand on the workpiece safely away from the blade. Other woodworkers keep both hands on the saw: one on the handle and the other wrapped around the front of the body or barrel of the tool.

JIG SAW SAFETY TIPS

- Do not use the saw if any of its parts are loose or damaged.

- Keep saw blades sharp, clean, and undamaged.

- Unplug the saw before changing a blade or making any other adjustments to the tool.

- Install a blade appropriate for the material you are cutting.

- Wear safety glasses and a dust mask for cutting operations that generate a large volume of wood chips or sawdust.

- To avoid vibration, support the workpiece as close to the cutting line as possible.

- Keep the saw baseplate flush against the workpiece during a cut.

- Keep your hands away from the underside of the saw when it is operating.

- Do not touch a blade immediately after using the saw; the cutting edge can become very hot.

- Make sure the blade is not in contact with the workpiece when you turn on the saw. Allow the blade to come to full speed before feeding it into the stock.

- Do not force the saw through a cut; this can snap a blade or cause it to veer off course. Allow the blade to cut at its own speed.

- Turn off the saw before backing the blade out of a cut.

- Make sure that any keys and adjusting wrenches are removed from the tool before turning it on.

- Stay alert. Do not operate the tool when you are tired.

CHOOSING A JIG SAW

All jig saws convert the rotary action of an electric motor into the up-and-down movement of a blade, designed to cut on the upstroke. Tool manufacturers offer three variations on this basic principle. On reciprocating-action machines—once, the standard for jig saws—the blade moves straight up and down. On orbital-action saws—now the most common variety—the blade moves slightly forward on the upstroke, then draws away on the downstroke. Many models feature both options, permitting you to choose either reciprocating or orbital blade movement. Orbital-action cutting was developed to make jig saws work more efficiently. By moving away from the workpiece on the downstroke, the blade generates less friction. The blade cuts quicker, but it enters the stock at a slight angle, increasing the risk of tearout and splintering. Hence, the greater the amount of orbital movement, the faster and rougher the results. Selecting the appropriate setting on your saw involves a compromise between speed and quality of cut.

A third type of saw is the scrolling model, which features a blade that can rotate in a complete circle within its housing, making the saw particularly well suited to intricate contour cutting. Aided by an edge guide, scrolling saws are also capable of making precise rip cuts.

Whatever type of saw you choose, one particularly desirable feature is variable speed, controlled by either trigger switch pressure or a separate dial. The added control allows you to match the cutting speed of the blade to the stock. You would generally use a higher blade speed with thicker stock.

CHOOSING A JIG SAW *(continued)*

Also look for a saw with a solid baseplate that will keep the blade square to the stock for standard cuts, and one that can be tilted up to 45° for bevel cuts. The tool should include a roller guide that supports the back of the blade as it cuts. Some models also feature a sawdust blower to keep the cutting line from becoming obscured, and on-tool storage of the blade-changing and baseplate adjustment wrench.

For fine cutting with reduced splintering, some models include a removable plastic insert featuring a slot that fits snugly around the blade. By bearing down on the cutting line, the insert helps to eliminate tearout on the top face of the stock.

JIG SAW FEATURES

Trigger-lock button
Locks trigger switch in depressed position for continuous sawing

Handle

Chip cover
Deflects wood chips and sawdust away from operator and cutting line

Trigger switch

Blade clamp

Orbital-action selector
Sets blade for reciprocating action and three different settings for orbital sawing

Roller guide

Baseplate

Circle-cutting guide
Pivot point at one end is driven into center of desired circle; other end locks onto saw baseplate. Distance between blade and pivot point equals circle radius

Edge guide
Guides saw for ripping. Arm locks onto saw baseplate; fence rides along stock

JIG SAW ANATOMY

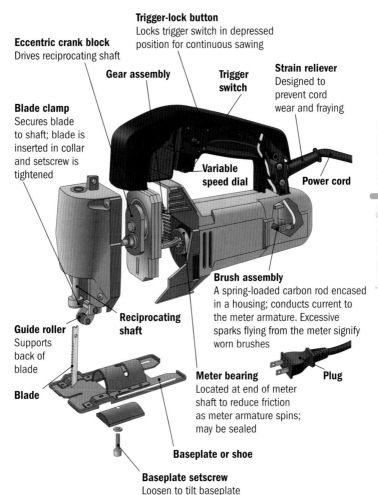

Trigger-lock button
Locks trigger switch in depressed position for continuous sawing

Eccentric crank block
Drives reciprocating shaft

Gear assembly

Trigger switch

Strain reliever
Designed to prevent cord wear and fraying

Blade clamp
Secures blade to shaft; blade is inserted in collar and setscrew is tightened

Variable speed dial

Power cord

Brush assembly
A spring-loaded carbon rod encased in a housing; conducts current to the meter armature. Excessive sparks flying from the meter signify worn brushes

Guide roller
Supports back of blade

Reciprocating shaft

Blade

Meter bearing
Located at end of meter shaft to reduce friction as meter armature spins; may be sealed

Plug

Baseplate or shoe

Baseplate setscrew
Loosen to tilt baseplate

CHAPTER 5

Jig Saw Blades

Although the results always reflect the skill you bring to a project, the single most important factor in working with a jig saw is selection of the proper blade.

Most jig (or saber) saws are supplied with a combination blade that works well for many cuts. Because the blades for a jig saw are relatively inexpensive—and tend to break frequently—keep an assortment on hand in anticipation of a variety of materials and situations. Page 55 provides a sampling of the blades that are available for the jig saw.

When buying a blade, pay particular attention to its composition, the number of teeth, the length, and width of the blade, and the method of mounting. Most blades are available in high-speed steel, but bimetal types—with high-speed steel teeth welded onto a flexible body—are more durable.

Designed for fine cutting, blades with a larger number of teeth per inch (TPI) create a relatively narrow kerf and less tearout, and cut slower than models with fewer TPI. Length varies from 1¾ to 12 inches, but the standard size is 3 to 4 inches long. Not all saws accept every blade length, so consult your owner's manual.

JIG SAW BLADES

Combination Blade
All-purpose blade suitable for most straight and curved cuts.

Offset Blade
Its design allows blade to cut flush to perpendicular surface; well suited for cabinet work and pocket cuts.

Blade Mounting Methods

Universal   Hook   Tang

Knife-Edge Blade
Also known as knife blade; toothless cutting edge designed to cut paper, cloth, or very thin wood.

Grit Blade
Toothless blade with tungsten-carbide particles bonded to cutting edge; suitable for cutting veneer.

Reverse-Tooth Blade
Cuts on downstroke to eliminate splintering on top face of workpiece; ideal for veneer.

Metal-Cutting Blade
Cuts veneer and thin plywood with minimal risk of tearout.

CHANGING THE BLADE

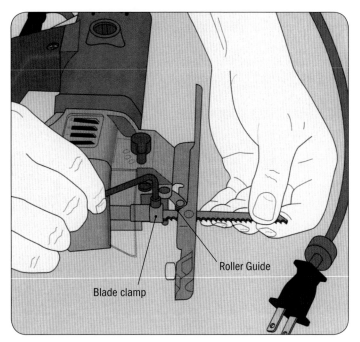

Roller Guide

Blade clamp

Unplug the saw, then set it on a work surface. For the model shown, removing the blade involves loosening the clamp setscrew with the hex wrench supplied with the saw and pulling out the old blade. (On some models, the wrench is attached to the power cord.) Insert the new cutting edge in the clamp with its teeth facing the front of the saw and its back seated against the roller guide. Tighten the setscrew.

SQUARING THE BLADE

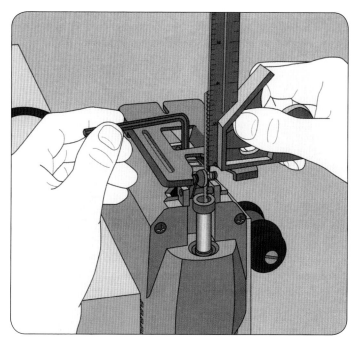

Square a jig saw blade each time you install a new blade. Unplug the saw, then secure it upside down in a bench vise as shown above. Use a combination square to check whether the blade is square with the baseplate. If not, loosen the baseplate setscrew with a hex wrench and tilt the plate until the blade butts flush against the square. Then tighten the setscrew.

Jig Saw Cuts

The jig saw is one of the most versatile tools you can own.

STRAIGHT CUTS

With a firm hand, a slow, steady feed rate, and a straight cutting line on your workpiece, you can make an accurate crosscut freehand with the jig (or saber) saw. Part of the attraction of this tool is it cuts quickly and with a minimum of setup time. For added precision, use an edge guide. The fence of the device is set for the appropriate cutting width, then the arm is fixed in place. You can also guide the saw with a straight edge, such as a board or a try square.

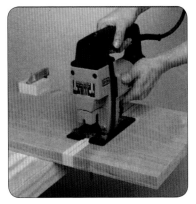

For best results making straight cuts, install a wide blade, especially if you are sawing through thick stock. Make sure the blade is long enough to cut through the wood in one pass. Resist the temptation to hold the stock with your free hand as you are cutting. Clamp the workpiece to a work surface, avoiding the risk of a spoiled cut or an accident.

A piece of masking tape applied along the cutting line will reduce splintering while you are ripping or crosscutting.

CROSSCUTTING

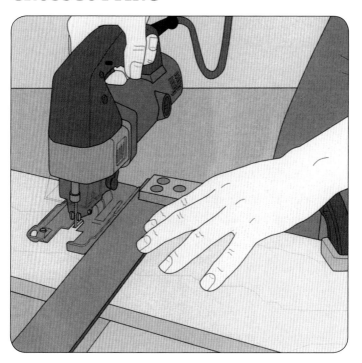

Clamp the stock to a work surface, arranging the board so the cutting line is beyond the edge of the table. Align the blade with the cutting mark, then butt one edge of a try square against the saw's baseplate. Make sure the handle of the square is flush against the edge of the stock. With the saw blade clear of the stock, squeeze the trigger. Feed the cutting edge steadily into the workpiece (above).

REDUCING SPLINTERING

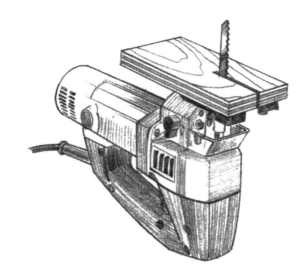

To reduce tearout, you can either saw stock with its good face down, score the cutting line with a utility knife, or cover the cutting line with a strip of tape. One other option is to install an anti-tearout jig on the underside of the baseplate. The jig is similar to the auxiliary shoe shown on page 61, but the notch for the blade is only as wide as the kerf of the blade you are using. The pressure the jig exerts on the stock will keep splintering to a minimum.

EXTENDING BLADE LIFE

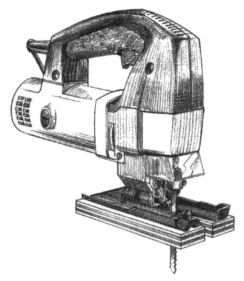

If most of the stock you cut is ¾ inch or thinner, the top third of your blade will be the only portion showing wear. To make better use of the full length of the cutting edge, install an auxiliary shoe on the baseplate of the saw once the top third of a blade begins to dull. To make the shoe, cut a piece of ½-inch plywood the same length as the baseplate and slightly wider. Hold the wood against the plate and mark the outline of the notch cut out for the blade. Saw out the notch and cut a slot for the blade. Screw the auxiliary shoe in place, making sure the back of the blade fits in the slot. (If the blade is not supported, it may wander and break when you are cutting.)

RIPPING

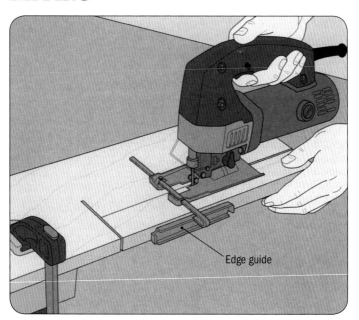

Edge guide

Commercial Guide

Clamp down the workpiece, making sure your cutting line is beyond the edge of the work surface. Install a commercial edge guide on the saw, then align the blade with the mark on the board. Butt the guide against the edge of the workpiece, then lock it in place. Holding the saw firmly, feed the blade into the board, making sure the fence stays flush against the edge of the stock.

RIPPING *(continued)*

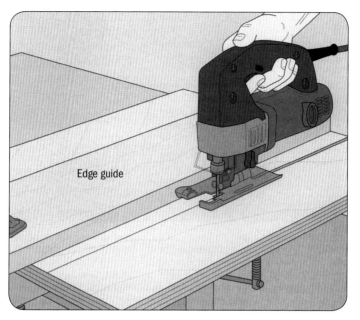

Edge guide

Shopmade Guide

If you are ripping a board too wide for a commercial edge guide, use a straight-edged board to keep the blade in line (above). The guide can be secured with the same clamps that hold the stock to the work surface.

MITER AND CROSSCUT GUIDE

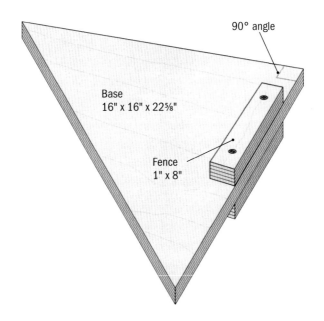

90° angle

Base
16" x 16" x 22⅝"

Fence
1" x 8"

The multipurpose edge guide shown above allows you to cut either 45°
miter cuts or 90° crosscuts with a jig saw. Make the jig from a piece of
¾-inch plywood, referring to the illustration for suggested dimensions.
Cut the base in the shape of a triangle with one 90° angle and two
45° angles. (To make a jig for 30° or 60° miter cuts, the sides should
be 12, 16, and 20 inches or a variation of the 3-4-5 ratio.) Screw the
fences to the base—one on each side—opposite one of the 45° angles.
The fences must be flush with the edge of the jig base.

MITER CUT

To cut a miter using the jig, set the stock on a work surface with the cutting line on the board extending off the table. Align the cutting edge with the line and butt the angled side of the jig against the saw's baseplate, with the fence on the bottom of the guide flush against the edge of the workpiece. Clamp the jig in place and make the cut, keeping the saw flush against the jig throughout the operation (above). To make a 90° crosscut, use the square side of the jig as your guide.

MITER AND BEVEL

The baseplate on most jig saws tilts to either side up to an angle of 45°, enabling the tool to make both bevel and compound cuts. Some models include a gauge that indicates the bevel angle, but you should always make a test cut to confirm the saw is set for the angle you need.

Because the saw blade will be in contact with more of the wood surface, use a slower feed rate when making angle cuts. For the same reason, it is generally a good idea to use a wider blade on the saw; a thin blade will be more prone to getting twisted. Although any angle cut can be made freehand, you will get better results if you take the time to set up an edge guide.

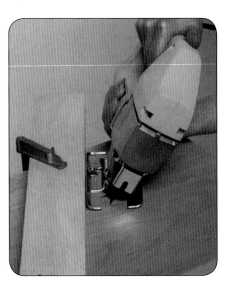

The jig saw makes compound cuts—sawing through a board with the blade presented at angles other than 90°–relative to both the face and edge of the stock. The cuts require two setup steps: (1) tilt the baseplate to the appropriate bevel angle and (2) clamp an edge guide to the workpiece to establish the miter angle you need.

MITER AND BEVEL *(continued)*

Miter with Protractor

Clamp the workpiece to a work surface, making certain the cutting line is clear of the table. Set a protractor guide to the angle you wish to cut, then align the saw blade with the cutting line. Place the ruled edge of the guide against the saw's baseplate; butt its other arm against the edge of the workpiece. Gripping the saw and protractor firmly, make the cut.

Protractor guide

Bevel Cut

Loosen the setscrew on the underside of the baseplate, set the blade to the desired angle, and tighten the setscrew. The setup and cutting procedure are the same as when you are ripping lumber with a shopmade guide.

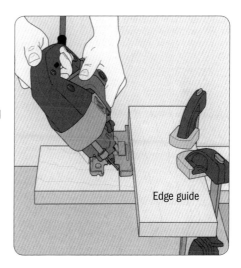

Edge guide

Miter and Bevel

CHAPTER 7

Jig Saw Curves

The jig saw is one of the few power tools adept at cutting curves. Whether you are a cutting a tight curve with a scrolling model, or using a standard orbital-action or reciprocating machine to form a gentle curve, remember to feed slowly. Cutting too rapidly can bend or break the blade.

Like the band saw, the jig (or saber) saw is useful for cutting circles. Although you can make such cuts freehand, both store-bought and shopmade jigs improve precision. In either case, secure the stock to a work surface. Depending on whether the circle or the surrounding stock will be the finished product, you can get the blade to the cutting line by making a plunge cut, boring a hole, or sawing a wedge out of the surrounding stock.

The best way to avoid binding when the edge of the workpiece is a short distance from the cutting path is to veer off the cutting line and saw to the edge of the workpiece; then come back and continue the cut at a gentler angle.

FREEHAND CURVE

To keep the blade from binding in the kerf, make release cuts from the edge of the workpiece to the tightest turns. Begin by aligning the blade with the cutting line at the end or edge of the workpiece. Feed the saw into the stock, guiding the tool slowly to keep the blade on line (top). For a cut like the one shown here, saw to the first release cut; once the waste falls away, turn off the saw. Resume at the next point where the cutting mark contacts the edge of the stock and work between release cuts (bottom). Complete the job by sawing back from the opposite end of the line to the final release cut.

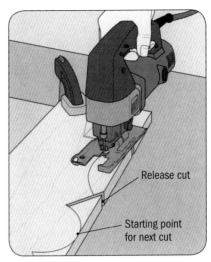

Release cut

Starting point for next cut

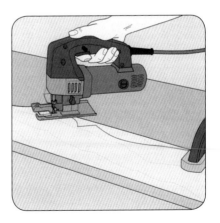

SCROLLING SAW

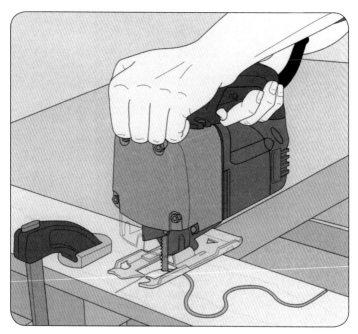

If the operation starts with a straight cut, feed the saw into the stock as you would a standard crosscut or rip cut. As the blade reaches the curved portion of the cutting line, release the scroller lock button, then use the scrolling knob to steer the cutting edge in the desired direction. Continue to the end of the cutting line, gripping the saw firmly with one hand and guiding it with your other hand on the scrolling knob. As shown above, steer the blade along a curved path by exerting moderate steering pressure on the handle.

RELEASE AND TANGENT CUTS

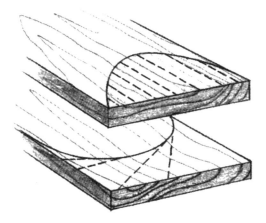

Depending on the curve you are cutting, you may need to straighten out the jig saw blade during the cut. Otherwise, you risk binding the blade in the kerf. For a curve leaving a concave arc in a workpiece (top board), make a series of straight release cuts from the end of the stock to the cutting line. As the blade rounds the contours and reaches the release cuts, waste pieces will fall away, giving the blade room to turn. For a convex arc (bottom board), begin at one end of the cutting line, but as soon as the blade begins to bind, veer off to the edge, or end of the stock. Then return to the cutting line, continuing in this fashion until the cut is completed.

SINK CUTOUT

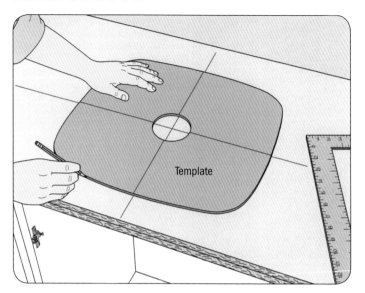

Template

Marking the substrate

Most new sinks include a template to help you position and mark the opening on the substrate. If you do not have a template, you can make one from cardboard. Place the sink face down on the cardboard and trace its outline. Next draw a second line ½ inch inside the first one then cut out the template along this inner line. Draw a pair of lines dividing the template in half both vertically and horizontally. Center the sink on the substrate atop its lower cabinet, marking intersecting lines on the substrate. Place the template in position and align the two pairs of lines. Trace the outline with a pencil.

SINK CUTOUT

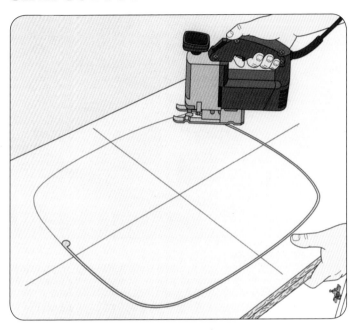

Cutting the opening

After marking out the position of the sink, check to ensure the line does not cross any of the screws holding the stretchers and cleats. Next, drill a ½-inch access hole through the substrate just inside the perimeter. Install a combination blade in a jig saw and lower the blade through the hole. Holding the tool firmly, turn it on and start cutting along the line (above). Try to cut as close to the line as possible. Tight precision is not required here because the sink's lip hides the edge. To keep the waste piece from breaking off as you near the end of the cut, support it with your free hand. Solid-surface tops should never be cut with a jig saw; instead, use a router with a straight bit and a plywood template.

CIRCLE-CUTTING GUIDE

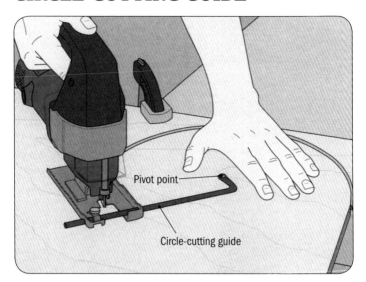

Pivot point

Circle-cutting guide

Using a commercial circle-cutting guide

Clamp down the stock with as much of the workpiece as possible extending off the table. Make sure the setup is steady, however. If the area inside the circle will be the waste wood, make a plunge cut or bore a hole (page 76) within the cutting line; if the material surrounding the circle will be the waste, make a release cut to the cutting line from the edge of the stock. Fit a commercial circle-cutting guide on the arm of the saw and drive the pivot point into the stock at the center of the circle you will be cutting. Adjust the guide until the distance between the blade and the pivot point equals the radius of the circle. Holding the saw and the stock firmly, cut out the circle (above). To avoid sawing into the work surface, turn off the saw and reposition the workpiece as necessary.

CIRCLE-CUTTING JIG

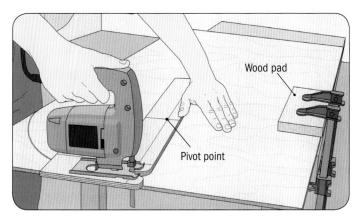

Wood pad

Pivot point

To cut circles exceeding the capacity of a commercial guide, use a shopmade jig customized for your jig saw. To make the jig, remove the blade from your saw and outline its baseplate on a piece of ½-inch plywood. Reinstall the blade and cut along the marks, making the section that will be beneath the baseplate slightly larger than the plate. Streamline the jig by trimming it down to the shape of an L, then cut out the notch for the blade. Screw the jig to the baseplate, ensuring the back of the blade is flush against the bottom of the notch. Next, use a pencil to mark a pivot line on the jig that is aligned with the blade. Cut into the stock to bring the blade up to the outline of the circle you will be cutting. Then drive a nail or a screw into the jig on the pivot line at the center of the circle. Cut the circle as you would when using a commercial guide.

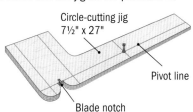

Circle-cutting jig
7½" x 27"

Pivot line

Blade notch

PLUNGE CUT

The jig saw's design makes it ideal for the tricky job of making interior cuts. Begin the operation in one of two ways: (1) use a drill to bore a hole or (2) plunge the blade into the workpiece, as shown below.

The second method made the cut quicker but is more challenging to perform. It takes some practice to keep the blade from skating on the surface of the stock. For best results, work with a short, stiff blade in the saw.

Make sure you have a firm grip on your jig saw when making a plunge cut, otherwise the blade will tend to jump off the surface of the wood at the start of the cut.

ShopTip

Boring access holes
An alternative to making a plunge cut in a workpiece is to bore a hole and insert the blade. Install a brad-point bit on a drill press or electric drill; the bit diameter should be wider than the width of the blade. At each corner bore a hole that just touches the cutting lines on both sides. Then insert the saw blade into the hole to cut to the adjoining corner.

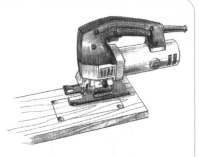

MAKING THE PLUNGE

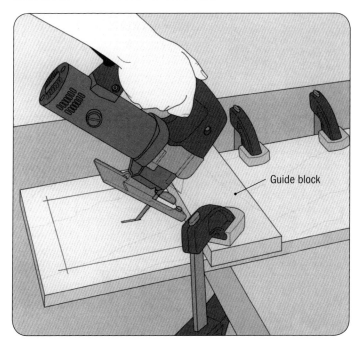

Guide block

Align a guide block with one of the cutting lines and clamp it in place as shown. Resting the front of the baseplate on the workpiece flush against the guide block, pivot the saw forward until the blade is above the stock. Then, gripping the saw firmly, turn it on and slowly lower the blade into the stock (above), keeping the baseplate butted against the guide block. Once the saw sits flat on the workpiece, turn off the tool.

COMPLETING THE CUT

Remove the guide block and continue the cut. To remove the bulk of the waste in a single pass, saw to one of the cutting lines. For the rectangular outline shown, follow the marks, but do not try to cut the corners square. Instead, bypass the corners with contour cuts (above), continuing until you reach your starting point and the waste piece falls away.

SQUARING THE CORNERS

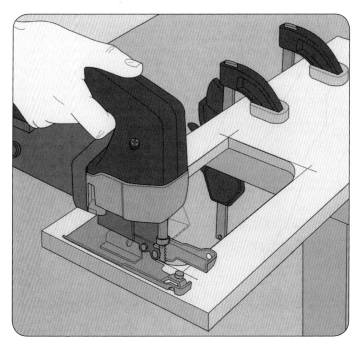

Cut away the remaining waste with two intersecting cuts at each corner (above). Holding the edge of the blade flat against one of the cut edges, saw along the line until the blade reaches the corner. Repeat this procedure on the adjoining side to clear the waste wood from the first corner. Then do the same thing at the remaining corners.

DUPLICATE PARTS

The jig saw lends itself to the production of multiple copies of a shape. Provided the stock is not too thick, stack sawing is an effective method for cutting duplicate pieces. Using this approach, layers of stock are fastened together and the pieces are cut in a single operation. Not only is stack sawing more efficient than cutting all the pieces separately, it ensures the finished products are exact copies.

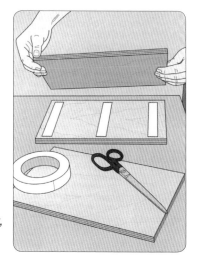

Some woodworkers use nails or screws to bond the layers together in preparation for cutting; others prefer clamps. Both approaches can be hazardous, however, if the blade accidentally strikes a fastener or clamp. A safer way is to use double-sided tape to hold the pieces together.

There are some limitations on stack sawing with a jig saw. First, the blade must be longer than the combined thicknesses of the workpieces. Depending on the model you have, you can buy jig saw blades up to 12 inches long, but do not attempt to use a blade that is too short. You will also probably need to make the cut fairly slowly.

Another option for repeat curved cuts is to use the first piece you cut as an edge guide for subsequent cuts. Clamping the guide to the workpieces can make a contour cut as straightforward as a crosscut.

SAWING THE STACK

Use double-sided tape to fasten the layers of stock together, making sure the ends and edges of the pieces are perfectly aligned. Mark a cutting line on the top piece, then clamp the stack to a work surface with the portion to be cut completely off the table. Align the saw blade with the line, then make the cut as you would for any other curve.

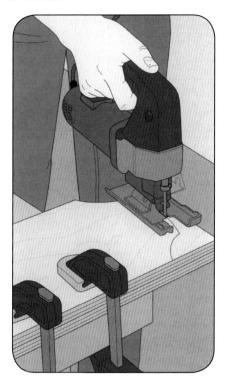

REPEAT CURVES

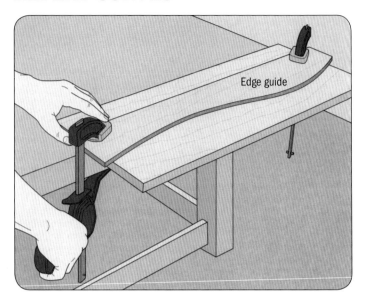

Edge guide

To cut a relatively gentle curve in several workpieces, saw the first piece freehand, then use it as an edge guide in making the others. Cut the guide slightly longer than the subsequent pieces to help in aligning the saw. Because the tool's baseplate will be riding along the guide, carefully sand the curved edge. Set the next piece of stock on a work surface. Mark a cutting line on its leading edge. Then align the blade with the mark and butt the edge guide flush against the saw's baseplate. Measure the gap between the back edges of the two pieces at both ends to make sure they are perfectly parallel, then clamp the guide in place as shown.

USING THE GUIDE

Masking tape

To help keep the saw directly on its cutting path, place a small strip of masking tape on the baseplate in line with the blade. To start the cut, butt the baseplate up against the edge guide and align the blade with the cutting mark. Feed the blade into the stock, keeping the part of the baseplate with the masking tape flush against the edge guide.

Index

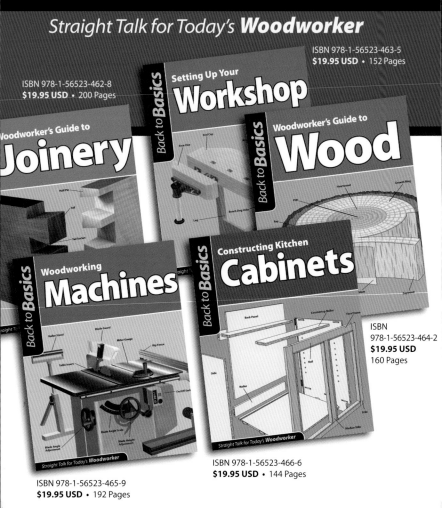

Back to **Basics**

Straight Talk for Today's **Woodworker**

ISBN 978-1-56523-463-5
$19.95 USD • 152 Pages

ISBN 978-1-56523-462-8
$19.95 USD • 200 Pages

Setting Up Your
Workshop

Woodworker's Guide to
Joinery

Woodworker's Guide to
Wood

Woodworking
Machines

Constructing Kitchen
Cabinets

ISBN
978-1-56523-464-2
$19.95 USD
160 Pages

ISBN 978-1-56523-466-6
$19.95 USD • 144 Pages

ISBN 978-1-56523-465-9
$19.95 USD • 192 Pages

Get *Back to Basics* with the core information you need to succeed. This new series offers a clear road map of fundamental woodworking knowledge on sixteen essential topics. It explains what's important to know now and what can be left for later. Best of all, it's presented in the plain-spoken language you'd hear from a trusted friend or relative. The world's already complicated—your woodworking information shouldn't be.

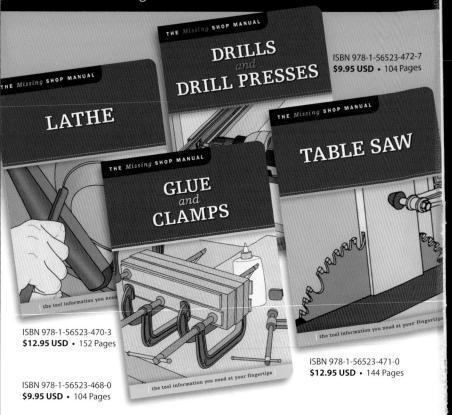